ARCHITECTURE ASIA

Journal of the Architects Regional Council Asia (ARCASIA)

T0284508

Editorial / 3

Jury Board / 4

Convener / 6

CONTENTS

A1 Single-family Residential Projects

Sabuj Pata / 8

A2 Multifamily Residential Complexes

Ras Houses / 12
The Statesman / 15

B1 Commercial Buildings

One Excellence / 20
CADG Innovation & Scientific Research Demonstration Center / 23
Arakawa Building / 26
DaiyaGate Ikebukuro / 29

B2 Resort Buildings

Navakitel Design Hotel / 33
The Aluminum Mountain / 36

B3 Institutional Buildings

Academic-Ark, Otemon Gakuin University / 40
Viettel Academy Educational Center / 46
Kokugakuin University Learning Center / 49

B4 Social and Cultural Buildings

Pocket Plaza, Yongjia Road, Shanghai / 54
UCCA Dune Art Museum / 60
Yan Luo Sports Park / 66
Agri Chapel / 69

B5 Specialized Buildings

Choui Fong Tea Café 2 / 74

C Industrial Buildings

The Architecture Wears PVC Pipes / 82
BingDing Wood Kiln / 85

D2 Conservation Projects: Adaptive Reuse

Dapeng Grain Warehouse Renovation / 90
Conservation and Renewal of Gunanjie Street Historic District / 96

E Integrated Development

Yan'an Tourist Service Center / 100

Special Awards: Sustainability

Pit Art Space / 104
Tea Leaf Market of Zhuguanlong Township / 107
Tank Shanghai / 110

EDITORIAL

The ARCASIA Awards for Architecture is an annual award established by the Architects Regional Council Asia. It aims to commend outstanding architectural works by Asian architects, encourage the inheritance of the Asian spirit, promote the upgrading of the Asian architectural environment, and enhance the role of architecture and architects in the social, economic, and cultural development of Asian countries.

This year, to manage with the challenges imposed by the Covid-19 pandemic, ARCASIA employed a different application and review process to call for entries and assess the submitted projects.

All projects were submitted by the applicants to a dedicated online portal where they were shortlisted by the jury. The portal opened to accept submissions from April 23, 2021 to May 22, 2021, and a total of 225 eligible submissions from fifteen countries, including some outside Asia, were received. A total of twenty-five projects were shortlisted and selected for the final review, which took place on August 28, 2021.

On October 31, 2021, the ARCASIA Awards for Architecture 2021 award ceremony was held in Starlight Little Theater, Nine Trees Future Art Center, Fengxian District, Shanghai. The Architectural Society of China undertook the evaluation and organization of the award ceremony and Professor Wu Jiang, Vice President, ARCASIA (Zone C) and Executive Director, Architectural Society of China, was appointed as convener and moderator. In accordance with the requirements of the city's Covid-19 prevention and control measures, the award ceremony was organized both online and offline, and only a small number of local shortlisted architects or their representatives from Shanghai were invited to attend.

Among the 225 eligible award-winning projects, five gold medals, seventeen honorary nominations, and four special awards were given out. As the organizer, ARCASIA was happily impressed by so many excellent projects, with their beautiful architectural forms and details that aptly conveyed the architects' sentiments toward a better, human-based living environment, as well as the built forms' consideration of urban regeneration and the intentions of serving the benefit of the broader public.

For example, Academic-Ark, Otemon Gakuin University, despite tight site conditions, creates rich and attractive spaces and adopts a passive energy-saving strategy; it also uses many modern technologies to achieve sustainability. The architects of Pocket Plaza, Yongjia Road, Shanghai transformed abandoned spaces into vibrant public spaces, creating a small community and a place for residents to gather; UCCA Dune Art Museum's subterranean structure fully responds to the surrounding beach environment; Choui Fong Tea Café 2 creates an open space with a wide view while interacting with the surrounding natural landscape and achieving an organic integration with nature; and in Dapeng Grain Warehouse Renovation, the old granary has been endowed with new functions and and a spark of vitality through limited intervention, making it a place where daily public and art activities occur.

This special issue of the magazine aptly ties together, and brings to completion the ARCASIA Awards for Architecture 2021. We take this opportunity to express our heartfelt congratulations to all the winners.

JURY BOARD

Rita Soh joined RDC Architects Pte Ltd in 1989 as an Architect and rose through the ranks to become Managing Director in 2016.

Over the years, she has played a key role in RDC's digitalization journey, making it one of the pioneers in the adoption of "information technology" in design and practice.

Adding to that, she also successfully led RDC to be the first design practice locally to achieve ISO 9000 certification in 1992.

Soh has been involved in the design and project management of healthcare, hospitality, residential, commercial, industrial, institutional, and infrastructure projects, both locally and overseas; many of these projects have won a variety of awards.

Soh is currently a member of the Appeals Board (Land Acquisition), and a board member of Sentosa Development Corporation, as well as the Housing Development Board. She is also a member of Mandai Development Committee and chairman of the Building & Construction Authority (BCA) Design & Engineering Safety Award Assessment Committee.

Her other titles include: President, ARCASIA (Architects Regional Council Asia); Chairman, SUTD Architecture & Sustainable Design Pillar Advisory Board; and Member, NUS Advisory Committee, School of Design & Environment. She was also formerly a Nominated Member of Parliament.

Soh holds a Bachelor of Arts in Architectural Studies and a Bachelor of Architecture (Honours) from National University of Singapore, as well as a Master of Science in Sustainable Building Design from University of Nottingham.

Kenya Hara is a graphic designer, president of the Nippon Design Center Inc., and a professor at Musashino Art University.

His highly influential exhibitin, RE-DESIGN: Daily Products of the 21st Century, toured worldwide, and he has built a reputation for producing exhibitions and educational programs that bring focus to new values by aligning with directions that bring to the fore theme words like "Haptic," "Senseware," and "Ex-formation." Much of his work, including the programs for the Opening and Closing Ceremonies of the Nagano Winter Olympic Games and works in the promotion of Expo 2005 are deeply rooted in Japanese culture.

In 2002, Hara became MUJI's art director. His wide-ranging work is noted for its attention to transparency, and also includes the visual identity design for Matsuya Ginza, Mori Building, Tsutaya Shoten, Ginza Six, and MIKIMOTO. From 2011 to 2012, his exhibition, DESIGNING DESIGN Kenya Hara China, was held in Beijing (its first station), and then expanded to Asia. In 2010, the House Vision program was launched to build a new platform for future industries; the Tokyo exhibition was held in 2013 and 2016, and the Beijing exhibition was held in 2018. The House Vision exhibition will be held in various cities in the future.

Hara also focuses on inspiring global interest in Japan, and served as chief creative director of the Japan House project for Japan's Ministry of Foreign Affairs. In July 2019, he launched the High Resolution Tour website as a new approach to tourism, exploring specific locations in Japan from an individual perspective.

Many of Hara's books have been published in English, including *Designing Design* (Lars Müller Publishers, 2007); *White* (Lars Müller Publishers, 2009); *Designing Japan* (Japan Publishing Industry Foundation for Culture, 2018); and *100 Whites* (Lars Müller Publishers, 2019).

Jitendra Singh is an architectural planner with over fifty years of experience that span his service in different capacities. He has taught at Indian Institute of Technology, Roorkee, National Institute of Technology, Patna, and Amity University Jaipur. He

became the first architect vice-chancellor of two universities in India—Jai Prakash University, Chapra and Nalanda Open University, Patna—and pro vice-chancellor of Patna University. He has held academic positions in leading institutes and guided the first PhD scholar from Patna University and Amity University Jaipur, respectively and has written over 150 research papers and four books.

There are many buildings to his credit in India. He has been active in the Indian Institute of Architects (IIA), The Institute of Town Planners India, and the Institution of Engineers (India) (IEI). He has been honorary editor of *JIIA* and reviewer of *IEI-Springer Journal* and *JIIA*, and also been a member of the IIA Council and the Council of Architecture—the statutory bodies of architects in India.

Professor Singh has held titles that include: Chairman, Sustainable Development Forum; Chairman, Architectural Engineering Division of IEI; Deputy Chairman, Education Committee of ARCASIA; and Member, Heritage Committee of the UIA (International Union of Architects).

Professor Singh received the Architectural Engineering Design Award (2004) from IEI, the Madhav Achaval Gold Medal (2005) and the Lifetime Contribution Award (2009) from IIA, the Eminent Architectural Engineer (2006) award, and the Amity Academic Excellence Award (2010) from Amity University Noida. He is a golfer, a past president of Rotary International, and is widely traveled, both in India and abroad.

Zheng Shiling is a full-time professor at Tongji University. He is a member of the Chinese Academy of Sciences, l'Académie d'Architecture de France, and a Honorary Fellow of the American Institute of Architects. He is also director of Institute of Architecture and Urban Space, Tongji University, member of the Academic Degrees Committee of the State Council, China, director of the Committee for Strategic Development, Shanghai Planning commission, and director of the Expert Committee for the Preservation of Historical Areas and Heritage Architecture, Shanghai. Zheng's other past professional titles include: Vice President, Architectural Society of China; President, Architectural Society of Shanghai; and Director, Committee of Urban Space

& Environment, Shanghai Urban Planning Commission. Now, he is director of the Committee for Strategic Development, Shanghai Urban Planning Commission and director of the Academic Board of Tongji University. Some of his main design works include: Nanpu Bridge, Gezi Middle School, Zhu Qizhan Art Museum, Fuxing High School, Nanjing Road Pedestrian Street, Shanghai, The National Finance and Taxation Museum, Hangzhou City, Zhejiang Province, and The Bund Public Service Centre, Shanghai (2013). He has published many papers and thesis in academic periodicals and journals, both international and within China, and also in international conferences. He has been the chair for many important juries for international and national architecture and urban planning competitions.

Francesco Dal Co is an Italian architecture historian. He graduated in 1970 from IUAV University of Venice, and has been director of the Department of History of Architecture since 1994. He was Professor of History of Architecture at the Yale School

of Architecture from 1982 to 1991 and Professor of History of Architecture at the Accademia di Architettura of the Università della Svizzera Italiana from 1996 to 2005. From 1988 to 1991, he was director of the architectural section at the Biennale di Venezia; in 1998, he was also curator of the architectural section. Since 1978, he has been curator of the architectural publications for publishing House Electa, and since 1996, editor of the architectural magazine *Casabella*.

In 2018 he curated the Pavilion of the Holy See at the 16th International Architecture Exhibition of the Venice Biennale of Architecture. The architects who designed the ten chapels were Andrew Berman (USA), Francesco Cellini (Italy), Javier Corvalàn (Paraguay), Flores & Prats (Spain), Norman Foster (UK), Teronobu Fujimori (Japan), Sean Godsell (Australia), Carla Juaçaba (Brazil), Smiljan Radic (Cile), and Eduardo Souto de Moura (Portugal).

CONVENER

Wu Jiang is a full-time professor at Tongji University's College of Architecture and Urban Planning. He was former Executive Vice President, Tongji University and former Deputy Director, Shanghai Urban Planning Administration Bureau, and was elected as a member of L'Académie d'Architecture de France in 2015. Since 2019, he has been the vice president of Architects Regional Council (ARCASIA). His professional titles include: Board Chairman, Global University Partnership on Environment and Sustainability (GUPES); Member, UIA Education Commission (EDUCOM); Vice President, Urban Planning Society of China (UPSC); Standing Council Member, Architectural Society of China (ASC); Director, Institute of Architectural Education, Architectural Society of China (IAE-ASC); and Chairman, Asian City Forum.

Wu has been invited to well-known universities and research institutes worldwide to deliver keynote speeches, including Harvard, Yale, and Princeton, as well as the departments and bureaus of urban planning and management in New York, Los Angeles, and Paris. He has also delivered keynote addresses at major international conferences, like UN HABITAT III and ACSP. He has been invited to be a juror at the final review of the Dubai Awards hosted by UN HABITAT. WU is also the founder of several joint international design studios with top institutions such as Princeton, HKU, ETH, Yale, UIUC, and TU Berlin. He was the curator of 2002 Shanghai Biennale Urban Construction, as well as the founder and chief curator of the first Shanghai Urban Space Art Season (SUSAS 2015). The latter is regarded as one of the most important cross-border big events spanning city, architecture, and art in China.

Wu is a devoted architecture scholar. His research fields cover architectural history, urban planning, and urban regeneration and urban governance. His portfolio also features the publication of several high-profile books, including *Elaborated Planning of Historical Streets: A New Perspective on Organic Urban Regeneration in Shanghai*; *Asian Cities: Planning and Development*; *Shanghai Urbanism at the Medium Scale*; *A History of Shanghai Architecture: 1840–1949*; *The Chinese Modern Architectural History* (5 Vol.); and *The History of Modern Architectural Education in China (1920–1980)*.

A1

SINGLE-FAMILY

RESIDENTIAL PROJECTS

Sabuj Pata

HONORARY MENTION

Location:
Dhaka, Bangladesh

Award credit:
ASIA KARIM, INDIGENOUS

'The past corresponds to the facticity of a human life that cannot choose what is already given about itself."
–Jean-Paul Sartre

The client, an artist by profession, sought a "sanctuary" for his family and yearned to relive a childhood that was spent among lush greenery. To that end, he found a place 21 kilometers away from the city center in Hemayetpur, Savar, where his children could grow among nature, experiencing its beauty. The building speaks through its porosity, to nature and its surroundings. Keeping the existing foliage and trees untouched, the building features an envelope so that the bare materials don't stand out as foreign against the existing texture of the land.

The house is divided into three parts: a three-storied block on the north and a two-storied block on the south, with an articulated triple-height space connecting the two; nature was a vital element to this thought process. The blocks unfold toward the south and south-east, so that every inch of space has room to breathe.

The frames of the balconies are constructed with steel bracing and wood planks to create a perforation to help nature pass through, as well as extend views to the bare earth below. The ground floor plinth is elevated to the extent that it subtly meets the bare earth, which seems to seep into the internal space. Creepers and trees cradle brick and raw concrete and allow leeway for wood and glass to make a path for the earth and sky. The rooftop holds a sanctuary—an elongated studio that makes up a serene space to excuse oneself from household chores and practice in peace.

A2

MULTIFAMILY

RESIDENTIAL COMPLEXES

RAS Houses

HONORARY MENTION

Location:
Rajasthan, India

Award credit:
SANJAY PURI

A series of low-rise volumes amidst open courtyards and landscaped gardens create sixty-one executive guest houses, forty-seven hostels for bachelor accommodation, and eighteen studio apartments. Located in Ras, Rajasthan, India, this development highlights a plan where internal spaces respond to the desert climate of the location. Deeply recessed windows, open and sheltered courtyards, naturally ventilated circulation spaces, and cross ventilated living spaces contribute toward reduced heat gain and naturally cooled interiors. Each part of this housing development is planned at the existing levels of a contoured site with contour differences of 3 to 8 meters, resulting in economy of construction and minimal cutting and filling of soil, which deliver a resultant height variation that creates character.

The organic layout of the housing is derived from old Indian cities with constantly varying scales and changing axis to create individuality for each part of the housing. Minimal intervention with the contoured site, low rise planning, facilitation of natural light and ventilation, reduction of heat gain, water recycling and rain water harvesting, local labor employment, fly ash bricks, and the use of residual energy from a nearby cement plant render this project economical and sustainable. The total area of 204,719 square feet was built within INR 1,300 (USD $18) for each square foot.

Color acts as an integral parameter in differentiating volumes, as well as in marking circulation spaces, while also alluding to the colors of the region. In Rajasthan, colors play an important role in the lives of the people, who also wear bright colors daily. Most cities in Rajasthan, too, are identified by color. For example, Jodhpur in Rajasthan is known as the blue city, with traditional homes in hues of blue lime plaster.

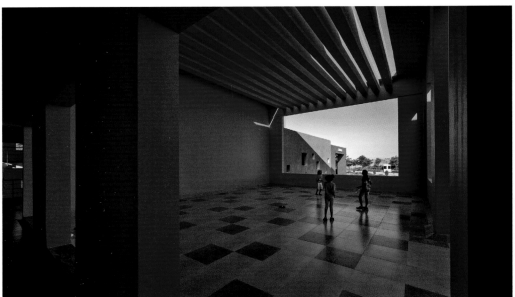

The Statesman

HONORARY MENTION

Location:
Dhaka, Bangladesh

Award credit:
Shahla K Kabir, Suvro
Sovon Chowdhury, Studio
Morphogenesis Limited

The inception of residential multifamily developments are mostly governed by their saleability. This project approaches this standard by questioning the development norms of such residences. Effort was made to motivate the developer to introduce some apparently unorthodox ideas—which were rather appreciated—and to show that the given standards for functional planning and material inventory are (somehow) devoid of innovation. The design strove to break the mold of the prevailing patterns for such developments, as well as introduce cutting-edge technology incorporated with novel functional planning. The resulting architecture is essentially modern in approach, comprising clearly defined public spaces with contrasting private zones.

Extrovert and introvert zoning of the plan translate to a prominent reflection on building aesthetic. The slender proportion of the built form evolves as two definitive shells, one being a glass box at the north—holding the public and entertainment zone in a generous bath of natural light—and the other, a screened box in the south that holds the private zone.

Long façades with reduced depth and very narrow façades with elongated stretch create challenging scenarios in achieving standard solutions for designing spaces and services. Both the functional arrangements of typical floors and vehicular and pedestrian movement at the ground are solved in unique modality. Through a simple solution of dividing the spaces into two to three zones, arranged along the circulations, a layered hierarchy of spaces is achieved instead of having segmented hierarchy.

B1

COMMERCIAL

BUILDINGS

One Excellence

HONORARY MENTION

Location:

Shenzhen, China

Award credit:

Farrells

One Excellence is the first major development in Qianhai, a vast new district in western Shenzhen that aspires to form an international business center rivalling Wall Street or Canary Wharf. For this pioneering district, the architects were tasked with developing a bold architectural design that anticipates urban integration with future surrounding developments.

Central to the scheme are the multilevel streetscapes, which create lively interplays between different functions to generate vibrant retail spaces. The development's design, which interlocks the towers and the streetscapes is conceived as an evolution from the imposing shopping malls and isolated towers that have dominated Shenzhen's urbanism throughout its initial decades of growth.

Green spaces, metro links, and multilevel circulation routes weave seamlessly into the pedestrian networks that connect the wider Qianhai district. The project features four office towers, including the 300-meter landmark tower and iconic 180-meter "gateway" towers, as well as two residential towers; each have a high level of demand from buyers and tenants. The "gateway" towers play an important role in shaping the emerging city by welcoming visitors and signifying the beginning of the next chapter in Shenzhen's unprecedented growth. Rich architectural features complement the permeable streetscapes and create a variety of diverse public spaces with character and purpose. These include an iconic gateway canopy and a residential clubhouse, as well as skylights, enhancing the urban experience throughout. The design embraces the development's coastal setting with soft tower forms and fluid cladding sculpted to mimic the flowing movement of water.

CADG Innovation & Scientific Research Demonstration Center

HONORARY MENTION

Location:
Beijing, China

Award credit:
China Architecture
Design & Research Group

In 1988, the restructured China Architecture Design & Research Group (CADG) was relocated to No. 19 Chegongzhuang Street from the southern annex building of the Ministry of Construction. Over the past twenty years, both newly built and renovation projects have been witnessed in the No. 19 compound, along with the development of CADG's office buildings, including the completion of the No. 2 office building in 2000, the completion of the No. 3 office building in 2002, and the renovation and façade upgrading of the No. 1 office building in 2010. In 2011, CCTC, the parent company of CADG, initiated the construction plan for the CADG Innovation & Scientific Research Demonstration Center (Innovation Center),

which was set to be located at the northwestern corner of the compound, where the former canteen, basketball court, and boiler room were situated.

Unlike the No. 1, No. 2, and No. 3 office buildings mentioned above, the Innovation Center has been planned as a multifunctional office complex with the former functional spaces on the site relocated within the building. Meanwhile, its openness to the city—a result of the demolition of the enclosing wall of the compound—is complemented with its highly comprehensive functionality.

Arakawa Building

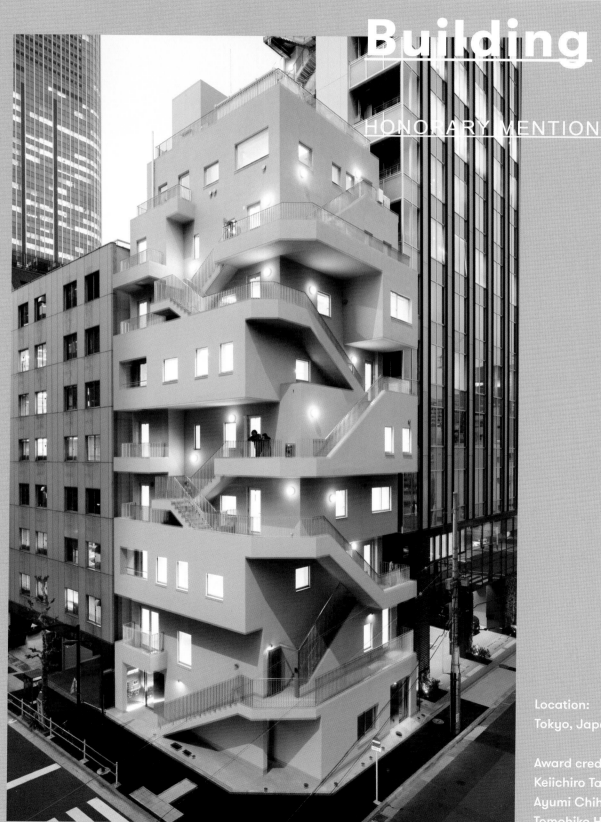

Location:
Tokyo, Japan

Award credit:
Keiichiro Taniguchi,
Ayumi Chihara,
Tomohiko Hayata

Arakawa Building was a project to rebuild the owner's office and residence, as well as the office space for rent on a street corner of Nishi-Shimbashi, Minato-ku, Tokyo's historic business district. Many of the mid-story rental buildings, which occupy the majority of Tokyo's commercial and business districts are now facing a rebuild. While the main streets near the site house large development projects like Toranomon Hills, the back streets make room for buildings of similar size to Arakawa Building.

The building has long contributed to its surrounding cityscape and the growth of the owner's business. In its rebuild, focus was placed on creating a building that would shape an attractive cityscape for the future; this was done by revisiting the potential of the building. The sculpted and modulated façade that exposes the emergency stairs plays a complex role in shaping the building's structure and controlling the environment, while also contributing to safety. Adding to that, it also provides an interaction between the city and the internal activities revealed on the surface.

The space supported within this façade is a regular-shaped space and is easy to use. As a result, it becomes an attractive workspace with an appropriate buffer from the outside. Arakawa Building utilizes the full potential of all building elements, while showing new prospects on how a mid-rise building, which is an essential element of any cityscape, can contribute to the city.

DaiyaGate Ikebukuro

HONORARY MENTION

Location:
Tokyo, Japan

Award credit:
Koji Okada, Sae Ito

Seibu Railway, the owner of this building, was established in Ikebukuro in 1912. Seibu Railway's corporate color is designed to express: safety and reliability as a railroad company; facing head-on the challenge of new things; and coexistence with the natural environment. The site of this project is where Seibu Railway began its operations and it is adjacent to Ikebukuro Station, the terminus station of Seibu Railway.

Against this background, this project began with three major missions: to design a 100-meter high-rise building featuring offices with the largest floor plates available in the area; to create a local landmark and a company headquarters endowed with symbolism; and to rebuild the station-centered pedestrian networks.

However, in order to take up 2,100 square meters to be one of the largest office floors in the area, the construction needed to cross the railroad. This would be the first time in Japan that a skyscraper straddles a railroad, and so, safety during construction and setting in place safety measures against earthquakes were required.

Next, to address all the issues, the construction process needed to follow and employ to the best advantage the guidelines set out in "Development Plans for Railroad Station Premises and the Collective Approval Process" in the comprehensive design system. The approach was for the building to straddle the railroad via a deck and to build on top of this deck. As this building is located in Ikebukuro, the terminus station of Seibu Railway, it stands as a symbolic gateway for the trains coming back to the station.

CHITECT AND
d)

China)

B2

RESORT

BUILDINGS

Navakitel Design Hotel

HONORARY MENTION

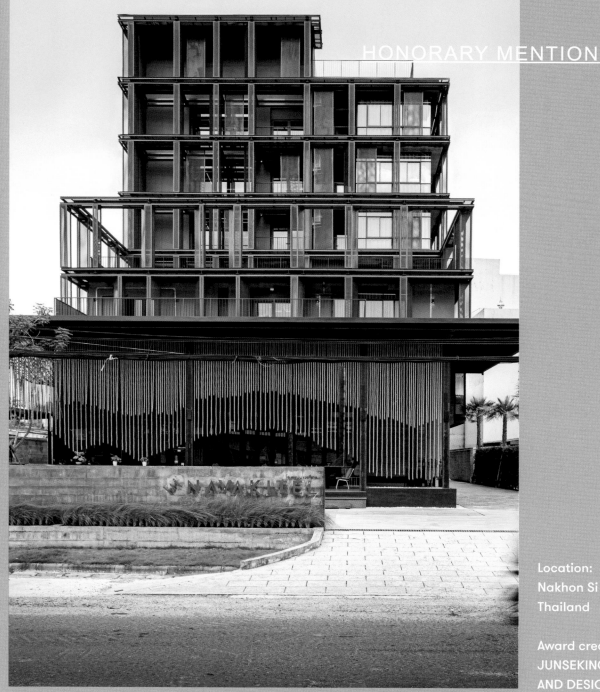

Location:
Nakhon Si Thammarat,
Thailand

Award credit:
JUNSEKINO ARCHITECT
AND DESIGN

The central part of Nakhon Si Thammarat, one of the most ancient cities in the southern part of Thailand, provides the location for Navakitel Design Hotel. The site is surrounded by shophouses and residences.

Navakitel Design Hotel consists of sixty-eight accommodation units, a lobby on the ground floor, and an open terrace on the third floor for organizing hotel activities. The intention of the project was to design an apartment with a reinforced-concrete structure. In order to transform the function of an apartment to that of a hotel, the architect decided to maintain the remaining building floor plan which had already been built up to the second floor. Based on the construction drawing, the room types are categorized according to their size, with each floor having similar room types.

Thin, sharp, steel plates on this seven-story concrete building diffuse the thickness of the building. By using a solid steel plate and expanded metal to create dimension and blur the solidity of the building, natural light is able to penetrate into the building. The architect also elaborately designs the building system in this project, which is usually neglected. Consulting with electrical engineers enabled the building system to be integrated with lighting installations and other equipment in the interior spaces, that span guestrooms, lobby, and corridors. Instead of concealing the building system within the gypsum ceiling, it is left exposed, and the result of the collaboration between architect and engineer become a part of the building aesthetic. With the expertise of local craftsmen, who include ironworkers, carpenters, and masons, their know-hows have been applied to the architecture and interior design in order to reflect the unique characteristics of Nakhon Si Thammarat in the hotel design.

The Aluminum Mountain

HONORARY MENTION

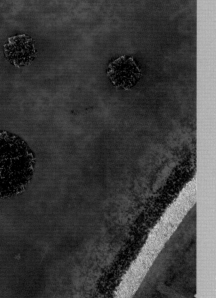

Location:
Huizhou, China

Award credit:
Wutopia Lab

The Aluminum Mountain serves as the Traditional Chinese Medicine Health Industrial Park Exhibition Center of Ping An Real Estate and Guangzhou Fangyuan Group. It is supported by six concrete columns.

In order to build this 880-square-meter center with a cantilever structure extending to 10 meters, thirty tonnes of iron truss were applied in order to shape the subtle and hovering peaks. The 11.9-meter spiral staircase is an independent structure traveling from the basement to the top.

The "sliver" aluminum board was decided as an ideal material for the mountain. In order to manipulate the heavy mass and texture of the aluminum material such that it is "dissolved," so as to provide a perfect foil for the lightness of the mountain, three different aluminium boards with perforation rates of 45, 60, and 70 are used, so that the mountain evolves from dense (at the bottom) to sparse (at the top). This creates an effect such that the mountain looks overwhelmingly heavy most of the day, but at night, with the lights on, it loses its materiality to be transformed into an enormous mountain of light. In this way, the mountain assumes an ethereal look.

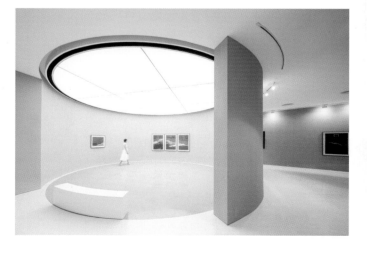

Gold Winner

- Yasuhiro Sube, Keisuke Aneha, Mitsubishi Jisho Sekkei (Japan)

Honorary Mentions

- VTN Architects, Nghia Vo Trong (Vietnam)

- Koji Okada, Toshimi Ura, Takahide Fukui (Japan)

INSTITUTIONAL

BUILDINGS

B3

Academic-Ark, Otemon Gakuin University

GOLD WINNER

Location:
Osaka, Japan

Award credit:
Yasuhiro Sube,
Keisuke Aneha,
Mitsubishi Jisho Sekkei

This campus design project played a core role in the redevelopment of a neighborhood in the suburbs of Osaka. Previously, the area was a jumble of factories, large apartment buildings, and single-family homes divided by a huge, walled-off factory site covering 18.5 hectares. The construction goal was to revitalize the neighborhood by opening up the former factory site to both students and community residents. With a timeline of just three years—from planning to completion—it was decided that a single-building campus that offers "live," in-person experiences, and which increases human interaction would be the best architectural response in today's era where the internet enables students the option of learning without ever stepping foot on campus.

A triangular-shaped volume is selected in order to reduce the shade cast on the surrounding streets and to avoid facing the building directly toward neighboring houses. In addition, the inverted-pyramid form with a library "floating" within, above a column-free indoor plaza, minimizes the building's footprint and, therefore, the time needed to complete excavations for archaeological artifacts prior to construction, as required by law.

The design concentrates activity within a central area, heightening the curiosity and excitement of students, as well as members of the community. This unique central plaza has a primitive appeal that gives students a sense of unity, while also serving as an emergency shelter and meeting place for the whole community. Although the building was designed to respond to future trends in education, it is equally relevant within the current Covid-19 crisis because it satisfies the universal desire for a place to meet and interact in person.

JURY CITATION: This is an interesting and challenging project with tight site conditions. Although there are many sharp corner elements, the architects have skillfully created rich and attractive spaces. The building adopts a passive energy-saving strategy and uses many modern technologies to achieve sustainability. The screen façade on the outer surface of the building lightens the environmental load in summer and creates a sunshade space with recognizable Japanese characteristics.

Viettel Academy Educational Center

HONORARY MENTION

Location:
Hanoi, Vietnam

Award credit:
VTN Architects,
Nghia Vo Trong

With an innovative design concept, Viettel Academy is one of the largest modern constructions built by raw bricks in Vietnam. Brick is a well-known local material and can be easily sourced at a reasonable price. Twelve blocks of building interspersed with breezy green gardens are linked by a large concrete roof system. Horizontal and vertical corridors create a rich interweaving of spatial dimensions and offer many interesting views. The pond, which is located in the center of the building acts as a reflective surface to emphasize the aesthetic of the brick material, and also generates a microclimate, as well as contributes to producing a cooling effect in the building. These harmonious design aspects form a unique semi-outdoor space where occupants can interact and enjoy being outdoors among nature. Not only does this innovative design answer the project brief, it also achieves a high expectation by harmonizing the architecture with its natural surroundings.

Kokugakuin University Learning Center

HONORARY MENTION

Location:
Tokyo, Japan

Award credit:
Koji Okada, Toshimi Ura,
Takahide Fukui

This project focuses on an annex to a Shinto (traditional religion in Japan that worships nature) university, which is built between a historic shrine and a residential area in the heart of the city. The aim was to open up the architecture to the history of the environment beyond the boundaries of the site, to create a comfortable place for students and a quiet living environment for the residential area—each with a differing character, but which build an overall sense of unity. By superimposing the three key design elements "extracted" from deciphering the environment—namely the winding wall, the curved roof, and the tilted windows—the design aims for the coexistence of the learning center and the residences, as they interact through channels of natural elements such as sunlight, wind, and views of the trees. The aim was to create a "learning center that stimulates the five senses" that responds to the history of the surrounding environment.

The building realizes a comfortable learning center that highlights the three key design elements inspired by the surrounding environment and the adjacent residential area, in the process also ensuring a comfortable living environment for the residents. The winding wall and the curved roof bring sunlight, wind, and views of the trees to the residential area, while at the same time create a variety of non-uniform places inside. The tilted windows help to manage the two height restrictions on the shrine side, while maximizing the floor space; they also connect the learning space with the rich environment of the shrine. In this way, the design breaks away from the formal, homogenous "classrooms and corridors" that are often found in Japanese school facilities and creates a rich learning environment that suits the learning style.

Gold Winners

- Shen ZHUANG (China)

- OPEN Architecture (China)

Honorary Mentions

- Ming Zhang, Zi Zhang, Original Design Studio TJAD (China)

- YU Momoeda (Japan)

B4

SOCIAL AND CULTURAL BUILDINGS

Pocket Plaza, Yongjia Road, Shanghai

GOLD WINNER

SOCIALLY RESPONSIBLE ARCHITECTURE

Location:
Shanghai, China

Award credit:
Shen ZHUANG

Taking the opportunity to renovate an old quarter, the Xuhui District government decided to dismantle two rows of shabby residences that posed a fire hazard and transform the site into a public urban space. The surrounding environment with many old residential blocks, including the nearby Yongjia Road incorporate a pleasant scale with luxurious greenery. Based on that, an open plaza with appropriate scale was selected for this project set within the Yongjia neighborhood.

Creating a space that was not only friendly and open, but which also maintained a territorial bond with the neighborhood created some challenge. It was also important to manage the open space easily and effectively. To meet the requirements, a small square fully enclosed with open galleries is created. The floor, which is 0.5 meters higher than the street tailors a sense of inclusion and territory; it also provides an elevated view of the street. A hidden fountain serves both as an attraction and

a soft management strategy to prevent grouped dancing classes and activities, which could destroy the quietness of the place. Shrubs measuring around 1.2 meters in height and an iron gate of the same height form a boundary along the pedestrian channel. The gate can be closed at night to keep the area safe and free of trespassers.

At the end of the plaza are two auxiliary rooms for small retail businesses. The open gallery adopts a timer-steel structure; based on the rational architectural form, dramatic details are added to grab public attention. In contrast with the warm tones of the red bricks, red square floor, timber structure, and rusted steel wall, the steel pillars are painted bright green to create a sense of relaxation. Today, more than two years after pocket plaza was opened, this ordinary historic site has transformed into a meeting point and beloved community center for people of all ages, occupations, and backgrounds.

JURY CITATION: Pocket Plaza is an interesting and unique project. The architects have used simple intervention to create a connection with the environment. They have skillfully transformed an abandoned space into a vibrant public space, creating a small community and a place for residents to gather. The jury unanimously agreed that the project deserves the Gold Award for Social and Cultural Buildings.

UCCA
Dune
Art Museum

GOLD WINNER

Location:
Qinhuangdao, China

Award credit:
OPEN Architecture

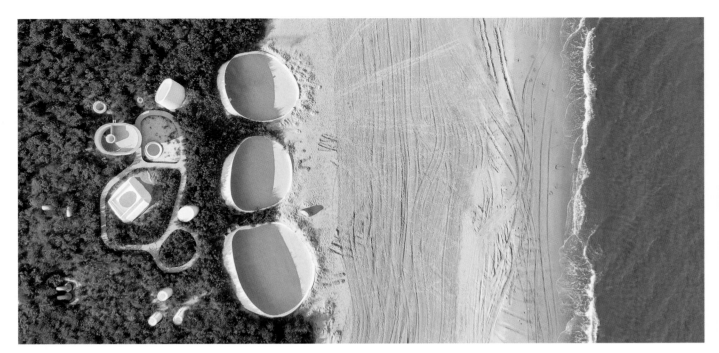

On a quiet beach along the coast of northern China's Bohai Bay, countless years of wind have pushed the sand into a dune several meters high. Carved into the sand, the Dune Art Museum lies beneath this dune, where it gently disappears. The simplicity and purity of the museum's design seeks a return to primal and timeless forms of space, and explores fresh possibilities for the experience of viewing art. A series of organically shaped, interconnected "cells," varying in sizes, face multiple directions to accommodate the museum's different programs, including galleries, a reception, community room, and café.

The client, the development company behind Aranya—an innovative seaside resort community located on the "Gold Coast" of Qinhuangdao in Hebei, China—wanted a great piece of architecture that would be attractive to its burgeoning clientele, who are mostly middle-class families craving a hide-out from exhaustive urban life. And so, the museum is tasked to bring art and culture into the lives of this somewhat utopian community. It is to provide both intimate individual and collective communal art spaces, and to have the flexibility of hosting community events. The completed building fulfills the design vision to create a sanctuary for both art and nature, and is simple, powerful, and touching.

From the time of its inauguration, this art museum has attracted a wide range of visitors from Beijing and beyond; it also opens up Aranya's otherwise gated community. At the same time, it successfully creates an engaging and non-traditional encounter with art—helping to promote the renowned UCCA art institution's rebranded mission of improving access to art through enriching and diversifying the visitor experience.

JURY CITATION: The UCCA Dune Art Museum is a unique building that shows the relationship between architecture and land. Its subterranean structure fully responds to the surrounding beach environment. In this museum, the relationships shared by architecture, people, and nature have been reconstructed, allowing us to get a feeling of the passage of time. It has been selected as the gold medal winner for this unique environmental experience.

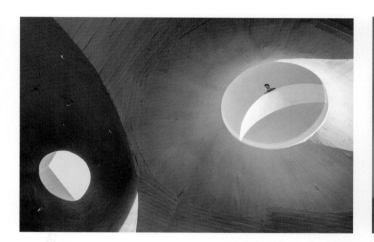

Yan Luo Sports Park

HONORARY MENTION

Location:
Shenzhen, China

Award credit:
Ming Zhang, Zi Zhang,
Original Design Studio
TJAD

Yan Luo Sports Park is located at a triangular site near a bend of the Mao Zhou River in Shenzhen. Situated at the edge of an industrial city, the site had become a construction waste yard surrounded by industrial plants and working-class dormitories, and was very much forgotten by the developed community to the north. At first, the intention was to change the area into a wetland park with simple sports facilities in the center. However, this decision was revised due to the site's isolated mode. Instead, an overlapping and staggered layout, with a raised corridor system surrounding several sunken depressions was proposed. In these depressions, different functions are introduced and include an urban square, sports ground, café, sports station, ecological wetland, and parking lots.

The main walking paths coincide with the corridor, providing shading space protected from harsh sunlight and rainfall. It, thus, breaks the cause-and-effect relationship between isolated buildings and the site they stand on. Rather, it rewrites the patch-like landscape between mountains and rivers in this area and also works as an ecological rainwater storage, while connecting the building more closely with the site by implanting various urban functions. The overlapping grid of the building extends in the direction of the city, providing an urban square, a parking lot, and other service facilities; in the direction toward the river, it integrates the wetland into the whole site, combining it with the cantilevered platform and gabion of the box-culvert embankment, forming a friendly green waterfront complex.

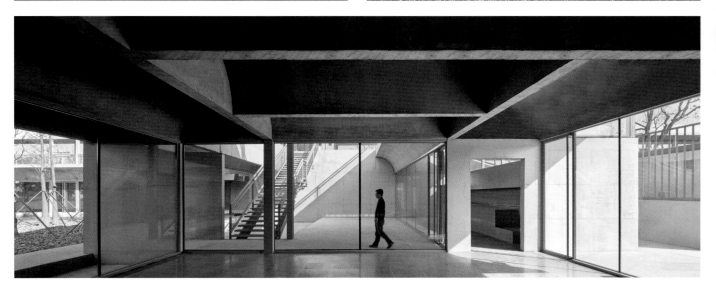

Agri Chapel

<u>HONORARY MENTION</u>

Location:
Nagasaki, Japan

Award credit:
YU Momoeda

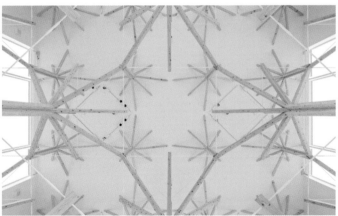

This is a wooden Japanese chapel with a fractal structure system. The site is surrounded by a large national park overlooking the sea and the activity of the chapel is seamlessly connected to the natural surroundings.

The oldest wooden gothic chapel in Japan stands in Nagasaki and is known as "Ohura-Tenshudou." This chapel is not only a famous tourist point, but also a place loved and cared for by the townsfolk. Agri Chapel is designed as a new gothic-style chapel using the Japanese wooden system. A pendentive dome is created by piling up a tree-like unit that extends upward by shrinking and increasing. Starting with four

120-millimeter square pillar units, the second layer is composed by eight 90-millimeter square pillar units, and the last layer by sixteen 60-millimeter square pillar units. A usable open space is provided by reducing the pillars at the floor level.

These tree-like units are constructed by the Japanese wooden system. The four corner bearing walls take on the horizontal force, and the inner wooden unit supports the roof load, which amounts to approximately 25 tonnes. The chapel also includes structural characteristics usually observed in gothic chapels: three-layered composition, nave/side corridor, and a 45-degree rotation, which integrates structure, space, and interior.

SPECIALIZED
BUILDINGS

Gold Winner

- Jeravej Hongsakul, IDIN
Architects (Thailand)

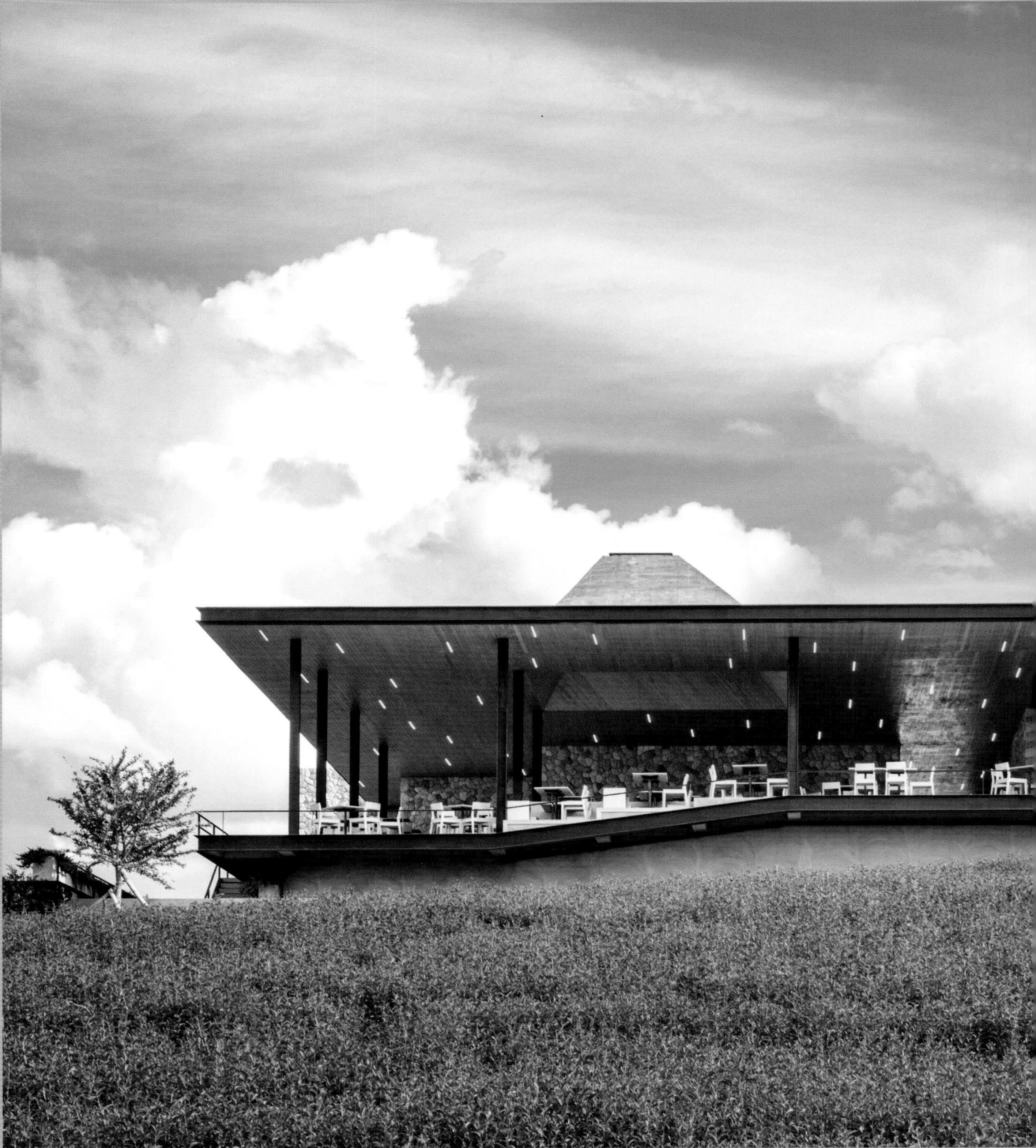

Choui Fong Tea Café 2

GOLD WINNER

GOLD WINNER

Location:
Chiang Rai, Thailand

Award credit:
Jeravej Hongsakul,
IDIN Architects

Since the first Choui Fong Tea Café began operations in 2015, the Choui Fong plantation has gained plenty of tourist attention and has become one of the most famous tourist attractions in Chiang Rai. Due to the excess of tourists in the first café, Choui Fong Tea Café 2 was established in order to serve the visitor surplus.

The second café is located on the plantation hill near the first. Prior to its operation, there were factories and retail outlets in the area; the new café replaces the retail belt near the factory, where a beautiful view lends its presence.

The project consists of a dining area with 250 seats, a large souvenir shop, and an exhibition area where staff demonstrate tea making, and where an exhibition shares the history of the plantation with visitors. The main concern in this project was in establishing a universal design, because through the long-established operation of the first café, it was discovered that family groups with elders are the main visitors to the cafés, and a universal design which serves that client base effectively would be the design of choice in the second café.

JURY CITATION: The project utilizes an interesting space design in the tropics, with a highly detailed building design. The building creates an open space with a wide view, while interacting with the surrounding natural landscape, achieving an organic integration with nature.

INDUSTRIAL BUILDINGS

Honorary Mentions

- KUK HYEON KU, Studio Atelier Maroo (Korea)

- AZL ARCHITECTS (China)

The Architecture Wears PVC Pipes

HONORARY MENTION

Location:
Asan-si, Korea

Award credit:
KUK HYEON KU,
Studio Atelier Maroo

PVC Pipe Skin (agricultural machine storage of Asan) is a building designed for the upcycling of PVC pipes that that are commonly used in everyday plumbing works. It has incorporated waste PVC pipes into the building structure to increase the efficiency of transparency, natural lighting, and natural drafts. This crossover not only increases the recycling of waste but also reveals the functionality of old PVC pipes as new design elements. This project has reconciled the functions and shapes for the given circumstances and uses through a PVC pipe façade design.

BingDing Wood Kiln

HONORARY MENTION

Location:
Jingdezhen, China

Award credit:
AZL ARCHITECTS

In the beautiful and tranquil hilly village of Qiancheng, the client Mr. Yu and his wife, as well as the local government, through the revival of the BingDing Wood Kiln, wanted to bring more attention to the Jingdezhen ceramic industry, as well as new opportunities for rural craftsmanship inheritance and economic development.

In traditional Chinese culture, porcelain vessels have not only served as a necessity in daily life, but they have also been an important container to hold the sentiments of life.

Gold Winner

- Ruiding Cai (China)

Honorary Mention

- Jianguo Wang, Architects &
Engineers Co., Ltd. of
Southeast University (China)

CONSERVATION PROJECTS:

ADAPTIVE REUSE

D2

Dapeng Grain Warehouse Renovation

GOLD WINNER

Location:
Shenzhen, China

Award credit:
Ruiding Cai

Located in the middle of Dapeng City, the granary was built in the 14th year of Wanli (1586), covering a total area of about 960 square meters. Its east-west axis is concordant with the spatial axis of the city; its west side is adjacent to the main street in the south–north direction of the city; and its north side is connected to the green yard of Xietai Yamen Site (the government office in feudal China).

The granary has only one floor, with ten rooms in total, and measures 42.5 meters in width and 22.5 meters in depth. Each room has a block arched roof and two vents. The load-bearing wall of the main structure is a wall of yellow mud, with a thickness of 318–327 millimeters. The cornice of the building is 4.0 meters high and the roof ridge is 5.5 meters high.

Except for part of the rooms, the building has been transformed into an exhibition hall for wooden boats; the rest of the space has not been used yet. The interior rooms are worn out and messy due to long neglect and disrepair, with the walls showing signs of peeling. As granaries are a key protection unit of ancient buildings, to adhere to the cultural relics protection law and fulfill other related requirements, only limited and slight interventions and adjustments have been carried out. The design combines the exhibition function to systematically comb and reconstruct the streamline, space, light, and courtyard.

JURY CITATION: The Dapeng Grain Warehouse Renovation project is different from the renewal and transformation of typical, traditional Chinese buildings. Guided by the desire to retain the original warehouse structure, the old granary has been endowed with new functions and imbued with a spark of vitality through limited intervention to create a place where daily public and art activities occur. This is a valuable case of building protection and renewal.

Conservation and Renewal of Gunanjie Street Historic District

HONORARY MENTION

Location:
Yixing, China

Award credit:
Jianguo Wang, Architects
& Engineers Co., Ltd. of
Southeast University

Gunanjie Historical and Cultural District at Shushan sits in Dingshu Town, Yixing City. Gunanjie, currently the most complete historical street from the Ming and Qing dynasties, was originally nearly 1,000 meters in length, but is now only around 400 meters long, and 2.4 to 3.4 meters wide. Buildings alongside the street are mostly one- to two-story brick-and-wood structures with well-preserved commercial storefronts, which are unique in their integrations with life and the production of the local rural lifestyle.

Gunanjie is both the birthplace and heritage of the Zisha culture. It is an epitome that embodies the development of Zisha. However, due to its long history, lack of preservation, incompleteness, and outdated facilities, Gunanjie was unable to meet the requirements of modern production. Losing this traditional charm, the district also faced pressure from residents to improve their quality of life. Hence, the design task was to research the protection and development strategies of Gunanjie, and to improve the living environment through construction and transformation.

INTEGRATED

DEVELOPMENT

Yan'an Tourist Service Center

HONORARY MENTION

Location:
Yan'an, China

Award credit:
Weimin Zhuang,
Hongjun Tang, Kuang Li

The project is located in the core urban area of Yan'an, extending to Baota Mountain Scenic Area, which is the most important tourist attraction in downtown Yan'an. Built during the reign of the Tang dynasty (618–907 A.D.), Baota Pagoda, which is set in this scenic area has been an iconic cultural monument in Yan'an for more than a thousand years. Unfortunately, due to the lack of holistic planning over the years, many cave dwellings were constructed in a disorderly manner on the hillside of Baota Mountain by local residents, which have severely damaged the appearance and ecology of the mountain.

Adding to that, in July 2013, the city suffered from an unprecedented, long and heavy rainstorm, which caused landslides and mudslides on a large scale. The mass collapse of cave dwellings in the scenic area and the risk of geological disasters in parts of the mountain endangered the architectural monuments in the area and the safety of surrounding residents.

In 2017, Yan'an launched the Ecological Restoration and Urban Renovation Program, and the Architecture Design & Research Institute of Tsinghua University was commissioned to conceive a tourist service center in Baota Mountain Scenic Area. The task was to accommodate functions such as tourist services, consultation, exhibition, and parking, and so on. This program was also intended to drive urban environment improvement in the region and set a pioneering example for the urban renovation and ecological restoration work in Yan'an.

When the project team was commissioned with the design task, the original buildings on the site had been removed, creating a scene of desolation. On top of that, the site is also surrounded by various historical monuments such as Star-picking Tower, cliff carvings, and a beacon tower, which needed to be protected.

- Ming Zhang, Zi Zhang,
Shu Qin (China)

- Yehao Song (China)

- OPEN Architecture (China)

SPECIAL AWARDS:

SUSTAINABILITY

Pit Art Space

Location:
Shanghai, China

Award credit:
Ming Zhang, Zi Zhang,
Shu Qin

Pit Art Space—from the coal-fired power plant reservoir to the art-sharing pit art space—is located in the Relic Garden of Yangshupu Power Plant, No. 2800 Yangshupu Road, Shanghai. Its predecessor was the deep-water storage pit of the Yangshupu Power Plant built in 1913, funded by British investment.

Pit Art Space consists of two deep pits in the north and south, connected by four 1.7-meter-diameter water pipes and is an important part of the industrial production link of the power plant. In 2015, with the launch of the entire Huangpu River Public Space Project, the power plant was shut down to implement an ecological and artistic transformation. By cutting off the connection between the pit and the Huangpu River and removing the building on top and the ceiling of the pit, the potential of the pit as a recessed underground building was stimulated.

The design preserves the historic thickness of the four walls of the pit, opening the connection between the deep pits in the north and south. At the same time, in order to change the inaccessibility of the original space, a new spiral steel staircase was installed inside the pit on the south side. The lightweight steel structure contrasts with the rough concrete texture of the pit wall. The artist-in-residence of the Shanghai Urban Space Art Season in 2019 created a unique artwork specifically for this space that perfectly matches the vibe and fits in the space form, turning the ambiguity of the pump pit into a natural art exhibition venue.

Tea Leaf Market of Zhuguanlong Township

Location:
Ningde, China

Award credit:
Yehao Song

Zhuguanlong Township is an important tea production town in Shouning County, with tea gardens that stretch 8.7 square kilometers. More than 90 percent of the people in Zhuguanlong Township are involved with tea production and the related industries. In order to standardize the tea leaf trade, it was important to build a centralized tea leaf trade market to undertake a variety of purposes—not only to provide standardized and professional places for tea farmers and tea merchants to carry out trade activities, but also to provide venues for holding various mass cultural and sporting activities. It was also required that the building be built quickly.

Tank Shanghai

Location:
Shanghai, China

Award credit:
OPEN Architecture

Along the banks of Shanghai's Huangpu River, five decommissioned aviation fuel tanks and the surrounding site have been given new life and relevancy. Over the course of six years, together with the newly created underground space and two standalone galleries, these iconic tanks were transformed from fuel containers into a vibrant new art and cultural center.

Conceived as both an art center and an open park, the project not only pays tribute to the site's industrial past, but also seeks to dissolve the conventional perceptions of art institutions with formidable walls and definitive boundaries that separate "museum goers" from "the person on the street." It sets out to be an art center for all, a museum without boundaries.

Program-wise, the project is very open-ended—right from the beginning in fact, with the clients and the architect considering and revising the brief many times in order to determine the most pertinent, sustainable, and viable use of the site. The diverse spatial configurations and the resilient and flexible design enable the center to adapt quickly, and allow the site to be used for many unplanned and diverse short-term events, such as art festivals, tech summits, fashion shows, and such.

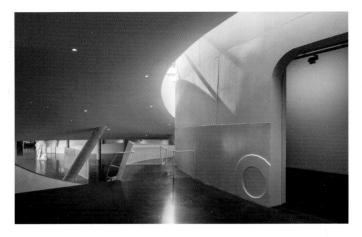